T0078335

I Remember Father Flanagan

I Remember *Father Flanagan*

CLIFFORD STEVENS

iUniverse, Inc.
Bloomington

I REMEMBER FATHER FLANAGAN

iUniverse books may be ordered through booksellers or by contacting:

iUniverse
1663 Liberty Drive
Bloomington, IN 47403
www.iuniverse.com
1-800-Authors (1-800-288-4677)

ISBN: 978-1-4759-9083-6 (sc)
ISBN: 978-1-4759-9084-3 (ebk)

Library of Congress Control Number: 2013908748

Printed in the United States of America

iUniverse rev. date: 05/16/2013

Contents

-1-

How I Met Him

I met him in a hotel lobby. I remember him as a tall figure coming down the stairs and meeting me with the kindest smile I ever saw, in my life. He was a famous man, and I was enchanted by this. He was Father Flanagan of Boys Town and I looked upon him with breathless wonder. I asked him that day if I could go to Boys Town and he listened to my story and took notes. He told me he would see. In two months I was on my way.

This was a familiar scene to Edward Joseph Flanagan. I was not unique either in the way I had met him or in the result of our meeting. This man had built Boys Town with boys like myself and he had built it with a touch of greatness given to very few men. With an idea, a dream, with a rare and magnificent courage he built a city of boys and caused a revolution. There were those who called him a crackpot and a dreamer, but the fruit of his work is there for all to see.

On a February day in the Hotel Brooks in Brattleboro, Vermont, I met him. It was only later that I learned his story.

He had not planned it this way, but he was destined for greatness. Even as a young priest, he was deep and different, and very bold. In the cold winter of 1913, he saw hundreds of homeless men walking the streets of Omaha. He went to a friend and together they found an old deserted garage on one of the back streets of the city. He bought a bale of hay and spread it on the floor of the garage. "You can sleep here," he told the men.

People instinctively came to him; he listened and did something. Those who called him impractical were those who were not interested, those who did nothing. He never looked at obstacles,

1

only to the deed to be done, then he did it in the simplest most direct manner.

In later years, a man told me: "I met Father Flanagan once, at a football game, I think. Then one day in Washington, D.C., he burst into my office. "I need twenty dollars," he said. I gave him twenty dollars. What do you do with such a man?"

At first it was the derelicts, the jobless and the alcoholics. He found a place for them to sleep, found them jobs, gave them food tickets. He made arrangements with grocery stores and restaurants and printed his own tickets. The news got around, tongues began to clack. He spent his time with odd specimens of humanity, and many did not like it. They told him so. The Flanagan temper flared; he told them to mind their own business. He did not preach, he did not defend himself. He simply acted. But it did hurt, and he mentioned in later years that his biggest critics were the good, the ordinary good people who could not understand. He let them go their way and he went his.

Soon there were more boys than men. He had pleaded in court one day for five boys . . . . and the judge had given them to him. He had five boys on his hands. Five boys he could easily handle. But after the five came two more, then eight more, the six more, then . . . .

Others could take care of the men.

But how to take care of them? Where to house them, they had no homes? Desperate to find a place, he was on a streetcar one day, telling anyone who would listen that he was looking for a house. "Ask her," one of them said. "She works for a real estate agent." She listened, then told him about a sturdy building on 25th and Dodge streets which seemed just what he was looking for. The rent was $90.00 a month . . . . in advance. "I'll be back tomorrow" he told her. "I have to see a friend." No one was ever sure who this "friend" was and there have been many guesses.

He got the house, but he needed more. Back to the young lady he went. "I need a Secretary to sort my mail and write my letters. How about coming to work for me?" The young lady, Catherine Shields Dannehy went to work for him and stayed with him until he died and became herself, a legend at Boys Town. Mrs. D., as her friends called her, knew more about Father Flanagan than anyone alive.

After I arrived at Boys Town in April of 1942, I went to meet the man who had brought me there. His office was on the northeast corner of the Administration Building. I climbed the short, steep stairway and walked back around a telephone switchboard, and past a row of offices. His was at the end. Mrs. Dannehy was at her desk in those days, just outside his door. She ushered me into that magic office.

It was magic because it was like the man it belonged to. Framed pictures of all sizes were hung casually and carelessly in an amazing abundance all over the walls. Some were or Babe Ruth or Lou Gehrig standing with Father Flanagan. Some were of Bette Davis or Joan Crawford with a greeting scrawled across the face of the shiny paper. Some were cartoons or news clippings. One showed Skippy kicking the dust and saying: "It's times like this when a fella wants to have a heart to heart talk with Father Flanagan." There was a whole series of Joe Palooka comic strips and in a special place of prominence on the west wall were autographed photos of Spencer Tracy, Mickey Rooney and Bobs Watson, stars of the movie "Boys Town".

"And how is the boy from Battlesboro?" he asked me (he never pronounced my hometown correctly). "O.K.", I said, and shook his hand. He rang a buzzer and a crisp little nun appeared, almost out of the wall. "Have you some candy for this young man, Sister?" he asked. This was Sister Electa, head of the Fiscal Department who was at Boys Town for many long years. In she came with a tin box filled with hard candies, and I took a modest handful.

"Are you happy?" he asked me.

"Oh, yes, Father," I answered

"You have every reason to be," he said. "Goodbye, dear"

That was all. Short and to the point. But I knew he knew I was there. Somehow that meant a lot.

At Boys Town, we saw him going and coming from his office. Sometimes he spoke to us, sometimes he did not; often he was absorbed in thought. He was planning greater things and no sooner were new buildings up at Boys Town than he was planning others. He sometimes let us in on his secrets at the weekly "conference".

3

This was held each Sunday at 11:00 a.m. in the morning. These were very informal, very chatty, and, at times, very pointed talks. He told us about the future of Boys Town, about the boys who had gone through Boys Town before us, of his hardships, of his disappointments, of the things at Boys Town he did not like, and anything that was on his mind. Then, for long periods of time, he would be away; and we would hear that he had spoken in Boston, or New York, or in the Senate at Washington.

Father Flanagan was a very poor preacher, but as a speaker, he was unsurpassed. In a man to man talk, he had no equal. When he spoke to you, his piercing eyes under thick eyebrows, studied you eagle-like. When he laughed, the whole room rocked with his laughter, and when he was angry, he was like a bull. He was never angry very long, and quickly forgot why he was angry. He knew more than any man alive about boys, yet confessed to be constantly puzzled by them. It is rumored that he once said, "There's no such thing as a bad boy—but they sure can be ornery."

The phrase, "There's no such thing as a bad boy," expressed the conviction upon which Boys Town was built and was a whip he used in his battle with those who lacked compassion. He never advocated a weak-kneed philosophy in dealing with youth as any Boys Town boy will testify, but lack of compassion in adults made him white with anger. He became a defender of the weak and helpless.

But that was only part of his work. He had a basic respect for youth; he seemed to have the conviction as few men have had it that the boy of today is the man of tomorrow. This was not just a slogan, it was an insight. He was not working just to solve a social problem or improve a social situation. That is why many social experts and people trained in social work failed to understand anything about the man. He had an interest in the individual boy, and he found each one amazingly different. He realized that in their hands rested the destiny of the world. With such a vision he worked, mightily and with real genius. He knelt in awe and reverence before this thing called boyhood, and he could not understand anyone who did not do the same.

-ii-

Father Flanagan in those days was away from Boys Town a lot. Sometimes it was to go and plead for a boy in trouble, sometimes to carry on a dialogue on youth work with professionals like Ruth Benedict and Attorney-General Tom Clark, sometimes traveling with the Boys Town football team.

I graduated from Boys Town in May of 1944, in a ceremony in the Boys Town Chapel. In a solemn ceremony, I received my diploma from Father Flanagan. At a class banquet earlier in the year, as class poet, I had expressed my feelings in this high moment of my life.

> *"One last glimmering candle, burning, burning, but not wholly done; One last song of parting, why must there be but one."*

Father Flanagan shook my hand and congratulated the boy from "Battlesboro", and I proudly clutched my diploma.

Since I was in no hurry to get myself settled in a job, I stayed around Boys Town for a few weeks after graduation, most of my friends having already left to get jobs or enter the Army. I left Boys Town for a few weeks for a visit back home, took a job briefly, but after a couple of months, took the train for the West Coast to join my Boys Town friends at the Mare Island Shipyards in Vallejo, California to do our share in the war effort. Since they had arrived before I did, they met me as I got off the train and found a place for me to stay. It was a strange kind of comradeship now, all of us out of school and working at a job, but still very close friends who would travel several miles to meet another Boys Town alumnus.

In November, the Boys Town football team came west, and the Boys Town contingent from Mare Island went to San Francisco to see the team play Black Hawk Military Academy in Kezer Stadium. We went first to the hotel where Father Flanagan was staying, met a lot of other graduates, and finally went out to the stadium to watch the game.

I made the mistake of sitting beside Father Flanagan during the game, and between the high moments of the game, he began to quiz me about my plans for the future. I had no definite plans, of course, but I did not want that bear-like look of his to grill me too deeply, so I said:

"Well, Father, I've been thinking about Maryknoll and maybe I'll go down and take a look at their seminary in Mountain View."

"Well," he told me, "if that doesn't work out, why don't you come back to Boys Town? I know you're interested in writing and I'll send you to any school in the country you want to go to. You can start at Creighton in Omaha, and from there you can go to Columbia or Notre Dame or anywhere you want."

The suggestion and the offer bowled me over. "Anyplace I want?" That opened up a lot of possibilities.

"Maryknoll might work out," I told him. "I'll let you know after I go there."

"Don't wait too long," he told me.

I did go down to Maryknoll and did talk to one of the Maryknoll Fathers in San Francisco, but I wasn't really serious about it and, as time went on, I began to turn my mind to other things.

The following June, I received a letter from Father Flanagan encouraging me again to return to Boys Town and begin my college studies. After much reflection and turning the matter over in my mind, I decided to follow his advice. My other Boys Town buddies were dispersing; one to the Navy, one to the Merchant Marines, and others to their hometowns or other jobs.

By mid-August, President Roosevelt was dead and the war in the Pacific was won. On the day the war ended, all the whistles blew at Mare Island and everyone left work, crowding into ferries that brought us to the mainland. San Francisco was in an uproar as servicemen invaded the streets celebrating the end of the war, the whole city in a turmoil for a couple of days. Vallejo was a bit more subdued, but we all knew that the end of an era had come.

I felt that an end of an era had come for me, too. I wrote to Father Flanagan and told him that I would like to enter Creighton University in the fall. He wrote back and told me to return to Boys Town anytime. I had no definite career in mind and it was decided that I would enter the College of Arts and Sciences at Creighton. Once again, I would be a resident of Boys Town.

I Learn About Him

The Flanagan family were tenants on a farm owned by an English landholder on the edge of the little village of Ballymoe in Ireland. The village was just across the River Suck in County Galway, but the Flanagan farm was in County Roscommon. The farm even had a name, Leabeg, so much was it part of the Flanagan existence. The father, John Flanagan, ran the farm with the help of his many sons and daughters, eleven in all, among whom were Patrick, who early in the life of the future Father Flanagan went off to the seminary; Nellie, who was a second mother to the younger members of the family, and Eddie, the youngest boy, born on July 13, 1886. The mother, Nora, was the dominant influence in young Eddie's life and he always consulted her before making any major decision.

The influence of his family upon Eddie Flanagan was profound, deeply woven into the very fabric of his thinking. It was a large family, each member a marked and distinctive personality, each one shaped by the tenderness and tensions of family living. Through all his years, Father Flanagan was strongly bound by ties to his family, and Boys Town, in a sense, from the beginning was a family project. What is important is that the warmth and tenderness of the Flanagan temperament which became the style of the man, the wit and child-like wonder that endeared him to many, and the resilient toughness and bear like brusqueness known so well to state officials and juvenile authorities was the product of Flanagan family living.

During the critical and competitive years of adolescence, however, Eddie Flanagan was far from hearth and home at Summerhill College in Sligo, a preparatory school of the Diocese of Elphin, on the northwest coast of Ireland. Here, he would be surrounded with the most historic and most beautiful landscape in all Ireland. Sligo was a port city, open to the Atlantic Ocean, with ships coming and going all the time. For him, it was the entrance into a larger world, quite different from the pastoral life at Leabeg. Here, he would show himself to be a remarkable student, graduating in three years.

During his early years, before going to Sligo, his brother, Pat, who had attended Summerhill College before him, left for the seminary in Dublin, and Nellie had gone to New York. Two older sisters of the family had left home and married. An old grandfather, deeply loved by the whole family, died. When his three years of schooling at Summerhill College was over, Nellie returned from New York with glowing accounts of life in the New World. After a long family council, it was decided that Eddie would continue his studies for the priesthood in America. The decision to become a priest had been made early and it was understood when he started his preparatory studies in Sligo that he would follow Pat into the seminary. The decision, however, was the young Flanagan's own. He returned to New York with Nellie on her return trip. Their brother, Pat, ordained the very year Eddie graduated from Summerhill College, had been sent to the Plains State of Nebraska and was already working as a priest in the diocese of Omaha. Within a few short weeks of his arrival in New York, the young Flanagan's studies were resumed at St. Mary's College in Emmitsburg, Maryland. He was just eighteen.

From the age of fifteen, Edward Joseph Flanagan was a student, and a singularly exceptionally one. But he had scarcely taken his first steps of formal training for the priesthood when he had to face the prospect of crushing defeat, something neither his mind nor his idealism was quite prepared for.

He found himself superbly equipped for his chosen vocation, and fired with strong and solid ideals, but again and again, three times in three years, his health broke and he had to accept almost complete failure. That the suffering and anguish of those years tempered in him that gentle toughness inherited from his family, there can be no doubt. It also concentrated his attention and his energies almost exclusively upon that inner world of thought and feeling which is the heart of the priesthood and gave him a lonely eminence and spiritual solitude that stayed with him until the day he died. This experience made him independent and decisive. It gave a cutting edge to his mind and manner and set him apart even in the Flanagan clan. This intense concentration of mind and energy upon his own inner world gave him just a touch of the contemplative. He acquired a strength and stability of spirit that helped him to face even more severe defeats later in life.

His final defeat during these years of preparation was a complete physical breakdown in Rome when the freezing cold and penetrating dampness of the Eternal City struck his body and withered his spirit at a time and in a place that made the whole experience cruel, meaningless and spiritually incongruous. With a tenacity born of sheer desperation, he clung to his hope for the priesthood. In his battle for health and for his chosen niche in life, he refused to be beaten down or turned back. He learned discipline and a ponderous patience.

Out of the darkness and near defeat of these black years, he came at last in 1909 to what he would consider in later years a near paradise, the bright and luminous atmosphere of the University of Innsbruck in the Tyrol of Austria chosen for its healthful climate and its scholarly traditions.

Here all the idealism that had been pent up in his battered spirit burst into flame and he worked with a calm and quiet energy that sharpened his mind and his spirit as the climate restored his health.

3. *Innsbruck: The Search for Identity.*

It is difficult to assess the effect of Innsbruck upon the young Edward Flanagan. His remarkable mind, unhampered by ill health and completely free of the regimentation prevalent in other seminaries of the time, recovered and strengthened a vision of the priesthood unconventional and bold. His contemplative bent found joy in his theological studies and drew from them a sense of identity that shattered any hesitation or fears that still clung to him from his years of defeat.

Hours alone on mountaintops (he became an expert mountain-climber and even joined an Alpine Mountain-Climbing

Verein) nourished in him a deep sense of prayer, and the freedom and personal solitude of those years made him happier and more contemplative than before. He would always have a peculiar attraction for high mountains and monastic solitudes and at one time even became convinced that his vocation was to be a Trappist monk. His contemplative gifts became tools for a rich priesthood and it was the vastness and nourishing peace of the Tyrol that the seeds were planted for the daring projects and experiments that led to Boys Town. The qualities of leadership which he consistently showed in later years (and the irritating "impracticality" which made him the despair of some of his contemporaries) were the fruit of a theological vision, ruthless and raw, acquired in the Innsbruck years.

In Edward Flanagan, the scholarship and brilliant intellect were always hidden under the humanity and compassion of an apostle, all his learning turned to love and he was never known for his academic knowledge of theologians and schools of theology. He could however, when the occasion demanded, bring forth from his arsenal of his mind, knowledge, facts and forceful reasoning shot through with a pragmatic sense which guided all of his work. Moreover, he clothed his theology in the humane literary tradition of Dickens and Canon Sheehan, and so his scholastic prowess was often hidden even from his closest friends.

The tranquility of these years never left him and the vision of his priestly work that he acquired at Innsbruck was the driving force of his whole genius. He always had a fondness for well-written books, especially of biography and history, which captured an idealism similar to his own, and he treasured the life or words of any man whose aim was a genuine nobility of life. He was never a man who lived by ideals alone, but he always remained essentially the dreamer who dreamed great dreams and then tried to make them come true. It was this solid Christian naïveté, profoundly theological and prophetically pragmatic, that was not quite understood by men of a more practical cast of mind. His insight and his intuition escaped them.

In 1912, he returned to his own people and to Omaha where his brother Pat had a parish and where his family now lived. Within a year, he would be swept up in a life's work that would draw upon all the energy and idealism he had so carefully stored away.

4. The Mission to the Men.

The first practical application of the idealism that drew him into the priesthood came in the summer of 1913 when Omaha was flooded with unemployed harvest workers, jobless because of a drought that had struck the Midwest. They poured into Omaha by the hundreds and the young priest met them on street corners and in back alleys. He began to organize a little campaign to help them and was able to get the cooperation of a few restaurants and grocery stores.

He ran into opposition and found that not everyone shared either his concern or his compassion. To him the issue was clear: What you do to others, Christ had said, you do to me. "Don't go to extremes," some of his fellow-priests told him, "You don't actually believe those homeless men are Christ?"

He did, and this was the crux of the agony this experience brought upon him. He could not fathom the thinking of those who did not take these words seriously and he proceeded to turn the whole city upside down to help the men. He begged, he borrowed, and he went into debt. And then he finally built a temporary home for the men in an old deserted hotel. He called it "The Workingmen's Hotel", but as he himself later wrote: "It was neither a hotel nor for workingmen; in reality it was a refuge for the down and out men loafing in the city during the daytime and sleeping in the parks at night." The harvest workers moved on when spring came, and a different kind of occupant took their place. At times he sheltered and fed as many as five hundred men in one night

It was discouraging, unrewarding work from every point of view. Except for the support of a few admiring friends and the members of his family, he was alone in the work. And his experience with the men made him realize he was helping them too late,

With the thoroughness he had acquired during his studies at Innsbruck, he made an exhaustive study of two thousand of the men came to the one startling conclusion: nine out of ten of them were the products of broken homes; their boyhood had been crippled by a lack of genuine love and the concern of responsible parents.

"I saw," he said, "that this waste of lives was preventable."

His Workingmen's Hotel also sheltered from time to time, a few boys off the streets. The similarity of the boys' home situation to the stories of the men was too terrifying for him to overlook. A search for other boys led him to the juvenile courts. Suddenly, unexpectedly, he had five boys on his hands. He found himself torn between two tasks, either of which would take all the time, money and energy he could put into it. Without hesitation, he closed the Workingmen's Hotel, and in another house in another part of town, Father Flanagan's Boys Home was born. Within a month, he had twenty boys and it seemed they would never stop coming.

5. Beginning the Work.

His second work was as unpopular as the first. The first years were crushingly unsuccessful and he barely managed to keep his little home open. Few citizens of Omaha saw any value in his efforts, and he was always desperately short of money and often of food. His boys were not welcome in the local schools and his odd mixture of races, religions and ethnic backgrounds was a source of scandal to many of the "better" families of the city. He was carefully and studiously ignored or avoided, a conspiracy of silence which left him quite helpless. At the blackest moment, according to a pattern he would follow for the rest of his life, he launched out into the unknown. He rented a larger home and moved his boys into their own "hotel", 'with a school of their own. With the help of a hard-working secretary, he began a campaign of publicity and correspondence that made him and his work known throughout the Midwest.

He became shrewd, clever and calculating as a fox. He watched the local newspapers for news of celebrities passing through Omaha. From that day forward his home became the mecca for the great ones of the country passing through the city. His name became associated with Jack Dempsey and Babe Ruth, with Will

Rogers and Tom Mix. His boys became celebrities in their own right and Father Flanagan lashed out at his critics with the carefully worded slogan that made him famous: "There's no such thing as a bad boy".

No one in Omaha believed it at first, but when he had said it often enough and Jack Dempsey and Babe Ruth and Will Rogers seemed to believe it, when his home became the stopping-off place for the great ones of the nation, the city took notice. He became respectable, but support for his work was still painfully small.

And boys came from everywhere: from Montana and Florida, from New York and Oregon—even from Mexico and Canada. Mothers left their baby sons and sometimes their baby daughters on his doorstep. Juvenile judges all over the country sent him boys who had been in trouble. Soon the two-story building that had once been a German-American Club was much too small. He tried to bargain and barter for a larger place, but no neighborhood would have him. Then one afternoon he took a ride in the country and told his small staff: "I just bought a farm out in the country. We're moving".

He did not want to leave the city, for he wanted to give his boys the opportunities that life in the city affords, but necessity drove him to a place where he could be completely independent. The isolation plus the vision of his work led him gradually to the concept of "Boys Town", but this would only be many years later when he had transformed the farm outside Omaha into a self-sustaining and unique little community. For years it was Overlook Farm and then Father Flanagan's Boys Home.

6. A Town for Boys.

At Overlook Farm in 1921, survival was the key concept. Two hundred boys were scattered through odd farm buildings over the hillside and Father Flanagan himself was housed, office and home, in an old garage. Despair crept into his bones as the boys increased and debts mounted and his family feared for his health. The news seeped into Omaha that the priest would have to close his home. There was silence in the city and then a growing sense of shame.

The man who had become a symbol of the city itself was failing because the city had failed him. The city rose up and in a mighty campaign led by its chief citizens raised over $200,000.00, and new buildings began to rise at Overlook Farm.

The Flanagan courage mounted the crest of the wave and he sent his boys on a fantastic circus escapade all across Nebraska, and in typical Flanagan irony penned another phrase that only half a dozen years before would have been meaningless to most of the people in the country: The Romance of the Homeless Boy. He had transformed one concept into a legend and from that day until he died he was occupied wholly in living the legend and making it live for thousands of boys.

Once he had changed the concept, he found himself fighting for individual boys and this brought him into ugly confrontations with state officials and juvenile authorities who did not share his convictions about the patently "bad boy": the boy who had killed or committed some crime of violence. To them the Flanagan conviction was criminal neglect itself and they resented the invasion of this "'soft-hearted" priest, who could bite hard words into their faces and whose learning and logic could be phrased in language that slashed at their dignity. He stripped the juvenile problem to its naked reality and his fierce reasoning made him a terrible adversary.

These were his years of concentration on the anatomy of juvenile crime, and his insights and intuitions showed him to be a master sociologist, psychologist and educator. Psychologists who had learned their business by clinical observation and scientific analyses of thousands of cases were amazed at the accuracy of his judgments and the superb skills he had developed. Yet this would always be hidden under the casual Flanagan manner; he never reduced his knowledge and insights to a system.

7. Boys Town.

Father Flanagan's total vision of his work found its full expression in Boys Town, in the concept of the boy, not as the ward of an institution or the inmate of a home, but as a citizen, still in a state of formation, but already possessing dignity and rights. The concept was at work very early when his collaborators were pitifully few and older boys were made responsible for younger boys, and the senior students were consulted in matters affecting the welfare of all.

He reversed the educational concept, prevalent in his own time, of a maximum of discipline and a minimum of freedom, and he gave every boy an atmosphere of genuine freedom, together with a backbone of discipline that led to a growing sense of responsibility. The revolutionary technique worked and Boys Town became a symbol of a new concept in education, and Father Flanagan became known as a superb educator. He labored in particular to keep his unique community from becoming institutionalized, for he dreaded the shadow of anonymity that clings to every institution and the facelessness of those who are confined within institutional walls. He labored to preserve for Boys Town and for every individual boy a sense of identity, and in doing so, his "City of Little Men" as it was called, became a unique addition to the legend of America.

In 1938, the legend became the common property of mankind when Spencer Tracy and Mickey Rooney immortalized Father Flanagan and Boys Town in the Metro-Goldwyn-Mayer motion picture <u>Boys Town</u>, The legend, too, reached out to new horizons in 1946 when Father Flanagan was asked by General Douglas MacArthur to travel to the Far East and assist him in rebuilding the youth of war torn Japan and Korea. On a similar trip to Europe two years later, Father Flanagan died in an Army hospital in Berlin.

To many he is still a legend, immoveable and immortal, like the stone statue of the man that stands in the middle of Boys Town, but to those who knew him, he was a rare and unique human being who, in his life and work, captured something of the greatness of man and reflected something of the greatness of God.

8. The Flanagan Mind: I

Father Flanagan was neither theologian nor philosopher and he did not articulate a carefully defined ideology. He was, in fact, singularly impatient with mere ideology and his gifts were rather prophetic and pragmatic. There was a tenacity to his convictions and an almost bull-like clinging to insights and intuitions that others regarded as platitudes. Beneath this dogged determination was a deeply-ingrained optimism, and what others sometimes regarded as sentimentalism was in reality a vibrant caritas, nourished and fed by theological vision that fired his whole priesthood.

From his school days at Drimatemple in Ireland, he acquired a fondness for books and always marveled at Dickens' grasp of the human situation. Oliver Twist remained for him the classic study of boy psychology and he found in David Copperfield insights that were an echo of facts in his own psychology.

He differed from others in the social work field in that he had no particular interest in "social reform", and was not passionately interested in improving social situations. He was interested in individuals, men and boys, and he had little patience with the generalizations and categorizing of the social work sciences. It was his experience that those heavily burdened with the scientific data of the social sciences often lost their common sense and looked upon a degree in their chosen field as a substitute for genuine knowledge born of experience. He abhorred especially the invasions of privacy which became the standard technique of certain schools of social work and his pragmatic optimism clashed with the casework mentality of many of his contemporaries. For these reasons, he was highly regarded by Individual-Psychologists, and one of his closest collaborators was the disciple and successor of Alfred Adler, whose child-guidance clinics in Vienna early in the century did remarkable work in the field of child psychology.

He consistently refused to be ideological. His habitat was not the realm of ideas. His whole philosophy was expressed in deeds and actions, not in words. He was existential in the best sense of the word, and it was in the white-hot arena of human affairs that his thought took root. His mind is best studied in his work, and Boys Town remains the monument to his thought and to his genius.

9. *The Flanagan mind: II.*

While the Flanagan mind was not ideological, he did have an appreciation for genuine scholarship and careful research. He enjoyed conversation with experts in any field and in reading good studies of biography, history or research. His library was a carefully chosen selection of works of good minds at their best and one of the great joys of his work was the association he had with men of stature in science, medicine, law, education and government. He himself could write with a pointed and fact-filled pen, as his report to General MacArthur on the youth situation in postwar Japan reveals, but he preferred dialogue to debate, and was at his best with the spoken word and face to face confrontation.

The rationale of his work was his own intellectual vision of human dignity and he saw embodied in the boy the whole human heritage from Aristotle through Thomas Aquinas. The sweep of the Aquinas' mind and its profound appreciation for solidly human and merely secular values was inborn in the Flanagan mind. Without this intellectual framework, carefully reasoned and deeply rooted in his thought, he might have been simply one more humanitarian fired by mere social compassion.

The vigor of his mind was evident in his public utterances when he carried on conversations with authorities like Ruth Benedict or Attorney-General Tom Clark and there are phrases in his report to General MacArthur that show him to be a careful and perceptive observer of the human scene.

His was a religious mind, but it is not loaded with pieties, and was singularly ecumenical long before the word or concept was fashionable. The Flanagan mind was tough and resilient, shot through with an unusual blend of theological and psychological insight. Upon this insight he built, not a philosophy, but Boys Town and his insight is embodied in a whole generation of boys.

10. *Father Flanagan the Man.*

From the elements of his history, we can construct a portrait of Father Flanagan the man. His was a mind with an instinct for innovation, a mind tempered to bold action and crushing defeat, a man willing to risk all on the strength of his own lone conviction. He was able to weigh well the complexities of the human situation and draw from them the simplicities which are the backbone of human motivation. He comprehended well the tension between public apathy and private feeling and he voiced in his own labors the disquietude of his whole generation. A disquietude, it must be remembered, which sparked the same generation in another part of the world and through the passionate vision of a man named Lenin created a far different social revolution.

His application of Christian principle to the concrete circumstances in which he moved and the moral fiber and intellectual insight he displayed were classical in the best sense of the term, and the superb artistry with which he maneuvered his work for boys into the public eye and changed in a few bold strokes of imagination the passion and prejudices of a whole generation suggest something more than mere priestly piety and Irish wit. Those who knew him knew the flint-like persuasiveness of his every uttered word, the hardness of his character and the depth of his feeling; his gift for friendship and his dog-like devotion to family and friends; the tongue that tripped on clichés and fed on platitudes; the gallant, uncalculating and sometimes mathematical mind; the swift, spontaneous and vigorous handshake; the insatiable appetite for work, the imperturbable confidence in the strange destiny that Providence had thrust upon him.

During his lifetime, by his style and by the magnitude of his own achievement, he created his own legend, a legend that is somehow larger than the man, and yet in some ways less than the spirit and vision that guided him.

The grain of his personality was a rare balance of humanity, insight and sheer nerve, coupled with an educated innocence that had looked deep into the inescapable tragedies of the human situation. He died in mid-century having straddled three continents in his labors. He left behind an imperishable memory and an example of faith and daring that antedated the aggiornamento of Pope John XXIII and the monumental achievements of the Second Vatican Council.

-3-

How He Worked

In the first half of the 20th century, the educational and religious work of Father Edward Flanagan was one of the most notable on the American scene and the institution that embodied it, Boys Town, became the stuff of legends. Boys Town was unique in the innate respect that Father Flanagan had for each individual boy and for his ability to fashion from the rough youth who came to him responsible adults who drew from him something of an inner vision that carried them through a lifetime.

His system was noted for a maximum of freedom and a minimum of discipline, at least that was the surface judgment, in radical contrast to other systems of education. But there was in fact a definite theory behind his work and it involved the creation of an organism, rather than an organization, mutual education on a large scale, where the influences for good were so many that very few who fell under his influence did not come off the better for it.

That was his genius. It was a careful molding of individuals by individuals, in a mutual give and take that was Boys Town. Some detected no system at all in his work, and others were severely critical of the slogan he made famous, crediting him with mere platitudes, if not rank sentimentality. But Edward Joseph Flanagan was no mean scholar and he approached his work with a thoroughness and intellectual acumen known only to a few. He discussed his views with anyone who wanted to listen, and those who listened were professionals and educators in their own right. According to one of them, Dr. Franz Plewa, who came to Boys Town from Alfred Adler's Child Guidance Clinics in Vienna. Father Flanagan was that rare human specimen who appears only once or twice in a lifetime, the intuitive genius, and Boys Town embodied the totality of his pedagogical vision.

His first asset was a superb education, crowned by his final years of study at Innsbruck University in the Austrian Tyrol, where scholarship was prized and where his mind was sparked with every vital current in European thought. He had been trained to think through problems, to sound out difficulties and to see until he found a solution. In the first work he tackled, a refuge for men off the streets, he was no mere doler of charity who provided bed and a free meal. He made a survey of 2,000 of the men who came to him and concluded that he was working at the wrong end of their lives. Without hesitation, he looked to the streets, and there found his life's work. From the beginning, he saw possibilities, and from these possibilities he fashioned the work that was at hand.

He saw every boy as the raw material for greatness, he saw what was possible, and somehow that rubbed off on the boys who came to him. He made it impossible for a boy to get into trouble, the peer pressure was in the opposite direction. He gave the boys a "town" of their own, something of pride and something of personal possession, of which each one was a vital part. Boys Town was the unique creation of a man who understood the meaning of community, of belonging, and of a contrived culture where education was total.

In contrast to most educators, he did not just devise a system of education or found an institution; he created a culture, a culture where the values he cherished and the goals he wanted his boys to have were living currents of the culture. He was not merely trying to solve a social problem, and most social scientists did not understand him. He abhorred the casework mentality of most social workers and depended on the organism to work, which it often did, miraculously, surprising even himself. Boys Town was mutual education in a planned environment where indefinable forces were at work: the indefinable influence of person on person, where freedom and individually were prized.

3. The Creation of a Culture.

The educational tradition that Father Flanagan drew on was as ancient as his homeland and pre-dated every other system in Europe. Whether he reflected on that or, not, he never indicated, but it is reflected in his work. The ancient Irish system of fosterage was unique in the ancient world and became part of the Celtic monastic system when Christianity arose in Ireland. It was based on a huge respect for the innate originality of each child and began by establishing the child in total freedom. It was gentle, immersed the child in play, and drew out of the child's own inner genius its own rich and unique potential. The system always centered around one beloved figure who gathered his charges around him and fashioned bonds with them that lasted a lifetime.

In his work at Boys Town, Father Flanagan was determined to break the back of the educational system that said education must be forced, that morality was inculcated chiefly by fear of punishment, and that education could flourish only in a system of constraints and strict discipline. He knew this was not true from his own experience and he knew it was not true from the Gospel of Jesus Christ. His educational system came from the Gospels, but he backed it up with a support system that touched every base in the boy's personality. He embodied his principles in a living culture, a culture of his own making, drawing upon a humane tradition that had achieved miracles in the past and had transformed whole peoples, leaving behind a rich cultural legacy.

What he saw as he entered upon his work was a social crisis, in which the homeless child was almost a surplus commodity, a religious crisis, in which character was molded by restraint, and an educational crisis, in which mass education was the norm. He rejected all of these, and inaugurated a social, religious and educational revolution that took the world by storm, making Boys Town world-famous, and the name "Father Flanagan" a household word. Not everyone could say what the name symbolized, but people came from all over the world to learn what the symbol stood for.

His most significant insight was that human beings are fashioned by culture, followed by another: that the human person

21

develops its full potential in an atmosphere of freedom and total acceptance. These two insights, coupled with the Christian conviction that the Gospel must not be forced, either in its propagation or its development, gave Boys Town a measure of success that drew the admiration of educators the world over.

3. *The Recovery of Christian Paideia.*

The innovative work of Father Flanagan cannot be captured in conventional categories because he outclassed them and went beyond them. Moreover, he rejected most of their tenets. His scientific analysis of their failure included the fashioning of hardened criminals in correction facilities and the shattered lives of the men who sought refuge in his shelter. Educational theories were for the well-to-do middle class, were often devoid of compassion, and were burdened with an insensitivity to social justice and moral responsibility. What was lacking was any insight into that elusive moral quality called character, which he looked upon as the heart and soul of all true education and the burning center of anything resembling pedagogy.

In the Omaha of his day, his educational vision included the Black child, an outcast in the urban vision of his day, where a mounting racial crisis would explode twenty years after his death, shattering the complacency of the city which ignored the injustice of its civic and educational policies. His most dedicated supporter was not a Catholic layman or prominent Catholic family whose wealth might have underwritten his labors. It was a Jewish businessman and fighter for social justice, Henry Monsky, head of B'nai B'rith, who recognized in Edward Joseph Flanagan something of the passion of Isaiah and the zeal of a Jeremiah and an ecumenical vision that embraced every human being in its concern.

What Monsky also recognized was something rabbinical in Flanagan's aphorisms and insights, a Talmudic wisdom that Father Flanagan drew from his Irish heritage, summed up in his classical saying, "There's no such thing as a bad boy ". This was the hand of hope that the priest held out to every boy whose life he touched, the redemptive grasp he had of his priestly mission and the unflagging confidence he had in the strange role that had been thrust upon him. What awed all of his contemporaries, his co-workers and associates, was the sheer stature of the man in his vision of his work and the profundity of the grasp he had upon his own labors.

Boys Town was a living embodiment of a Christian paideia, in contrast to the Catholic education of those days, where indoctrination tried to overcome the hazards of a dominantly secular society. This "system" gets its strength from personal influence, in a living environment where the child is cherished and deeply loved . . . Father Flanagan knew that without the inner growth that comes from a growing sense of personal responsibility, Christian education is doomed to failure. In this he clashed with Catholic educators of his time for whom the very concept of Christian paideia was unknown.

It is not impossible that in his studies at Innsbruck, the young Flanagan was profoundly struck by the pedagogical genius of John Henry Newman's "Idea of a University", new editions of which were coming off the presses in the two decades after Newman's death in 1890. The lectures contained in this book were delivered to an Irish audience, and are salted with references to ancient Ireland, where education flourished. Newman's view of university education was mutual education on a large scale and his statements on the subject of education are quotable and memorable. It would be interesting to contrast Newman's Idea of a University with Father Flanagan's Idea of Boys Town. Except for the university setting of Newman's "idea", the concepts are almost identical.

4. An Evangelical Revolution.

What impressed Father Flanagan in his clashes with the society of his day was the almost complete absence of practical Christianity. His first effort in applying Christian principles to a social crisis was during the drought of 1913, which brought hundreds of jobless men to Omaha, stranded as harvests failed and men walked the streets with no money in their pockets and no way to get home. These men were not drifters, they were husbands and fathers of families, whose work had run out as a drought hit the Midwest in the middle of the harvest season, upon which they depended for their livelihood.

There was little concerted effort to help them, religious and civic organizations gave only lip service and it was only when Father Flanagan, like and Old Testament prophet, reminded the St. Vincent de Paul conferences of the city that to have surplus funds in their treasuries in such a time was bordering on mortal sin, was he able to enlist a few of their numbers in facing the problem. He bought an old hotel for the men to stay in and issued food tickets, appealing to his own family to help him. With this experience, he became disillusioned with charitable organizations of any kind or with any form of institutionalized charity. His evangelical efforts and insights looked solely to individuals and he always had a mistrust of the bureaucratic niceness of organized charities.

Evangelical insights and Christian activities that were not aimed at the individual he looked upon as illusory and false. The Gospel did not make demands of others, it did not require an effort at conversion to justify itself; it gave unstinting and without reserve, expecting no return but the benefit to another. It was not an evangelical triumph that was looked for, but the living of the Gospel in concrete deeds. It was serving Christ in the neighbor, in whom one saw the living image of God.

This was so revolutionary that the young priest found himself in lonely isolation from the start, and after a few vain attempts, he never depended upon conventional Christians in his work. He worked by way of identity of interest, with a superb trust in Divine Providence that baffled his critics. He could be pointed in his response to those who got on his bandwagon after his work became popular and attracted the attention of Presidents and other celebrities.

When the city of Omaha raised $250, 000, 00 to save him from bankruptcy after he had to leave the city from lack of support, he said frankly: "Why didn't you come to my help two years ago when I needed it? You're a little late in your generosity."

His evangelical revolution catapulted him to fame and made him one of the most familiar of national figures, few willing to follow him in the audacity with which he carried out the vision of the Gospel. He turned money down or returned it, if it seemed that he had unfairly appealed to someone's generosity. In Hollywood, during the filming of the movie "Boys Town", after a visit to the M-G-M studios, a group of stars, headed by Joan Crawford, invited him to a gathering of stars who pressed huge checks into his hand as they greeted him. Thinking he had taken unfair advantage of them, Father Flanagan returned the checks next day. When he arrived back in Boys Town, he found that the checks had been returned to him, with double the amount of the original donation.

It was this utter transparency and simplicity of design that gave some the impression that he was merely a kind-hearted, sentimental Irish priest, saintly, but not especially intellectually gifted. This mistake was also made by juvenile authorities and state officials that he often tangled with over some wayward boy. He was a formidable intellectual opponent, well-read and highly-informed on every facet of his work. In a radio debate with the anthropologist, Ruth Benedict and Attorney-General Tom Clark, it was clear who was the most intellectually astute of the three. He knew his field with a masterly grasp of principles and applications, with a brilliance of explanation that silenced others. He knew what he had achieved and he had a grasp of the social problems he was facing with a scope and clarity that was simply astonishing.

In the educational theory that he forged, it was the object of education that he concentrated on, the child with unlimited possibilities, not the textbook and casework child, but the boy with the tattered hat in front of him, the wounded, wayward youngster for which there were no educational categories. He had a solidarity with that child and that was Boys Town. There is an immediate context to his work that cannot be separated from the work itself and his theory is embodied in the work.

His theory was the unlimited possibilities he saw in that boy who just came off the street. The unleashing of those possibilities was the substance of his educational theory and the chief reason for his astounding success.

-4-

How He Became Father Flanagan

Father Flanagan died in 1948 in Berlin, Germany, on an assignment from the United States State Department to advise the government on youth problems in postwar Europe. Two years before, he had gone to Japan and Korea at the invitation of General Douglas MacArthur to advise him on the youth problems of Japan and Korea after the Second World War. He was the world authority on youth problems and his voice had been heard in the press and in the courts, on the radio and on street corners. It was a strident voice. It was well-known that he hated reformatories and workhouses, but he was more than an advocate for the neglected and homeless boy: he was a superb educator whose educational theories were embodied in his work, and though he could speak eloquently and convincingly on youth problems and their solution, it was his vision of human worth that was at the heart of his work, and he faced that work with more than priestly compassion and a helping hand. He had hammered out that vision, not only from the Gospel that guided him every step of the way, but from a deep penetration of the very object of his life and labors: the adolescent boy. His experience in the field was massive and unprecedented.

At the time of his death, thousands of boys from every race, religion and ethnic background had passed under his care and observant eye, and his mind had gathered data, recorded, not in casework files or statistical reports, but in millions of written words in his Boys Home Journal, and in hundreds of speeches given before audiences entranced by what he called "the Romance of the Homeless Boy".

He was a master craftsman, a peerless educator, and an intuitive genius who outdid a generation of educators and child psychologists by his experience and insights into what education of the young is really all about. But his knowledge was more than experiential. He had garnered his wisdom and insights from a 2,000 year old tradition of pondering the Scriptures and working out their practical application in the concrete situation in which one has to live, a methodology he mastered in his exposure to the writings of the ancient Fathers of the Church, and from a theological vision deepened over long years of prayerful study, begun as a boy tending sheep with a book in his hands.

I. The Irish Roots.

The mind of young Eddie Flanagan was opened very early (he started to school when he was only five). He was taught, first of all, by father and mother and a family of brothers and sisters (he was the eighth of eleven); then by a schoolmaster in the basics of reading and writing; then by the local priest who introduced him to Latin, Greek and French at the age of twelve,; then by his wide reading of contemporary literature like that of Dickens, Scott and Macaulay. These he packed into his jacket as he went out to tend the cattle and sheep on his father's farm, reading voraciously for hours at a time. Even at this young age, he would spend his free time with his father in the fields, needing exercise and outdoors because of his frail nature. He was considered the bookworm of the family and the amount of knowledge he gathered from this casual reading under corn stocks and on the peat moss was considerable. It was from these days that he acquired a passion for books by master novelists, historians, poets and experts in any field of learning, who opened doors and windows for his young mind.

The Celtic Revival of William Butler Yeats and a host of Irish poets, novelists and historians was in full swing as he reached his teenage years, and he was thoroughly familiar with this blossoming of literary genius going on around him. He was known to be a thoughtful young man, a bit of a loner because he dwelt somewhat apart, occupied with his own thoughts. He had a quick mind, and, according to his brother Pat, who tutored him when he was home from the seminary, his mind was like a sponge, always eager to learn. He was just fourteen when he went off to Summerhill College in Sligo, his mind hungry for knowledge and for the gift of words that went with it.

The most profound influence on his future work was the family intimacy at Leabeg House, the Flanagan ancestral home in Roscommon. He remembered the chimney corner in the kitchen where he would sit and think as a boy, a teakettle hung above the fire and tea always ready. There were always rumors of the doings of the Fenian Brotherhood, and he would certainly remember the rebel songs sung around the fire by passing strangers or neighbors who happened to stop by. Some of the songs were tragic and sad like "Boulavogue" and some were rousing songs of rebellion.

As he reached the age of ten, attending one of the so-called "National Schools" at Drimatemple, a few miles from his home, he would be reminded that it was a half century since the Irish Famine of 1845, which sent so many Irish youth to America.

It is highly possible that he was acquainted with the oral traditions of Great Blasket Island which were coming to light at this time, with the magic names of Peig Sayers, Tomas 0 Criomthan and Gobnait Ni Chinneide on everyone's lips. Undoubtedly, too, he would have been fascinated with the itinerant storytellers, the Seanachai, who were common in Ireland. They were welcomed in every home, but outlawed by the English and Irish gentry since they kept alive the rich literary, historical and religious traditions of the Irish People. By the time he entered Summerhill College at the age of fourteen, he would have been deeply imbued with the traditions of his people and he could look back over fifteen centuries to the heroes and icons who inhabited those centuries.

There is a certain originality of mind that comes from this kind of family life, because Irish family life at this time was under the heel of an oppressor-even the farm they lived on was not their own. The Irish are by nature poets and deep thinkers, with a gift for metaphor and mystery and the unusual turning of a phrase. They look at the world obliquely because they think long and hard at what they do and the conditions under which they live. And there is an Irish lore that has never died, a lore preserved and developed in the hedge schools that were so much a part of 19th century Ireland and in the homes and hearths where their outlawed religion and their love of freedom were kept alive by song and story and by the neighborhood ceilis that preserved traditions as ancient as Ireland itself.

The young Eddie Flanagan was not unaware of the history of his people and the decision to become a priest came from a desire to join a long list of local heroes whose names and achievements stretch back to figures lost in the distant past, but as familiar as the next door neighbors. There is no other country where names like Finbarr, Kilian, Ronan and Diarmuid are as common as John, Robert and James elsewhere. To the Irish, these are contemporaries, and are part, not of a distant past, but of a living tradition. Like them, he acquired a vision that is not only Catholic in the doctrinal sense, but Catholic in the way it looks at the world.

This explains, too, Father Flanagan's openness to boys of every race, religion and ethnic background. Although it pre-dated what we now call ecumenism, it was far richer and deeper than that, because it was not merely the toleration of another, it was reaching out the hand of friendship to everyone, as Father Flanagan would later express it "regardless of race, color or creed". It did not come from an emerging Catholicism in a dominantly Protestant country, as in the United States. It came from the Gospel roots of his own Irish tradition and made Boys Town unique in the Catholic education of the time. It pre-dated the rise of ecumenism in the Catholic Church after the Second Vatican Council as well as the stalwart work of John Courtney Murray on pluralism in American society.

His masters did not go by the name of Freud, Jung or Adler, although he was able to draw upon the experience of many masters in his chosen field. His masters were saints and scholars in his native Ireland with names like Columcille, Jarlath, Enda and Comgall, and from ancient pedagogical masters with names like Athanasius, Augustine, Basil, Gregory, Boethius, Leo, Dante and Thomas Aquinas. What he found in these masters was a wisdom lain idle for centuries and a pedagogical genius unmatched in human experience.

In his native Ireland alone there were remnants and ruins of hundreds of educational centers that made the Irish the schoolmasters of Europe. One is Clonmacnoise, less than thirty-five miles from his home, which, as a center of learning, lasted for over 1,000 years, until it was destroyed first by Vikings, then by the Anglo-Normans and then by the English. The remains and ruins of similar educational centers are scattered all over Ireland, in Scotland and the Hebrides, in northern England and in monasteries and federations of monasteries through France, Germany, Switzerland and the Balkans. And it is not insignificant that many of the universities of continental Europe were founded by Irish scholars.

What is not widely known is the effect that the Latin Vulgate had on the emerging peoples of Europe after the fall of the Roman Empire. Many of these emerging peoples, like the pre-Christian Irish, were illiterate, and the effect of the Latin Vulgate upon these emerging nations was astonishing. It created, first of all, a culture of literacy that produced an explosion of poetry, art and literature. Secondly, it created a humanism that established, not only new institutions of learning, but hospices and hospitals and every form of social action answering every human need.

That was because the Latin Vulgate, in a language understood by everyone, brought new images to the mind and new sounds to the ear. It provided the intellect with an inexhaustible store of insight and knowledge, a symphony of new words and concepts, powerful prescriptions for right living, and a new charter of human relationships: personal, social, familial and political. And the Irish enshrined this Latin Vulgate in illuminated manuscripts of incomparable beauty, where this Word of God had a setting worthy of its dignity as the Word of God.

What is often overlooked is that classical education was flourishing in Ireland when it was dying on the continent and it was Irish scholars like Marianus Scotus, Virgilius of Salzburg, John Scotus Erigena, St. Columbanus, and a host of others, who brought classical learning back to the continent after the Barbarian invasions had devastated Europe. And that tradition had never died in Ireland. It was carried on, not only in the seminaries and in the locally run Irish schools, but in the homes and hedge schools and parish rectories, where scholars of the stature of Patrick Augustine Sheehan of Doneraile instructed private students in languages and in the classics. It was his brother Pat who introduced him to Letters, enabling him to skip three grades in the educational ladder, but it was the parish priest, Father Hughes, who tutored him in Latin, Greek and French.

When his young mind began to open to the wider world of learning at Summerhill College, he was ready for the vast world of Catholic and continental scholarship so aptly described in Newman's "Idea of a University", and to the tough meat of philosophical reasoning he would find at Emmitsburg, Dunwoodie, Rome and Innsbruck. Education even then, in the secondary schools of Ireland, was based on the Trivium and Quadrivium of classical education, even though that may not have been the designation given them in the school curriculum.

When Archbishop Farley of New York and Bishop Scannell of Omaha looked at the scholastic record of the young Edward Joseph Flanagan, they were truly astonished at what they saw. One sent him to the Catholic seminary at Emmitsburg, Maryland, where he earned his college degree in two years, and the other sent him to Capranica College in Rome and to the Royal Imperial Leopold Francis University in Innsbruck, Austria, where he could tackle studies equal to his talent. What he encountered at Dunwoodie, Rome and Innsbruck was a veritable ocean of knowledge, which he plunged into rather intemperately at first. This affected his health and nearly cost him the priesthood, but gave reasoned support to every human instinct he had fashioned in his growing up years, and opened to him the vast possibilities of priesthood and of a future that he would not only inhabit but would create.

2. The Catholic Roots.

The Flanagan mind was a unique combination of a profound theological vision, an uncanny grasp of pragmatic possibilities and the courage and ingenuity to explore those possibilities. With a boldness unprecedented at the time, he created a religious, educational and social model from a small body of empirical data, interpreted markedly different by others in the same field. He saw clearly, as the vision of Boys Town became a reality, the failure of almost every other model on the horizon, and he rejected most of the conclusions on the youth problem that were articulated in the professional journals of the time.

In stark contrast to others in the field of youth work, he was guided by a religious and theological vision, one that he had hammered out in the days of his early studies for the priesthood and in the luminous days of his studies at Innsbruck University. There, in the quiet and serenity of the Tyrolean Alps, he drew upon insights into human behavior and human nature from the rich theological sources of a Patristic and Thomistic renaissance.

The Patristic renaissance was based chiefly on the seed studies of the early Church Fathers by John Henry Newman, whose writings at the time had become classical, with names like Athanasius of Alexandria, Basil of Caesarea and Gregory of Nazianzus. These three in particular had created on the foundation of a rich Greek classical world, a Christian culture of astonishing richness and depth, where a Christian vision of human worth and possibility inspired social and educational experiments that transformed the Roman and Byzantine world.

Far more significant, because closer to him in time, was the revolution in theology brought about by Pope Leo XIII in his restoration of St. Thomas Aquinas as the author and propagator of a humane intellectual tradition, with insights into the roots of human behavior and motivation, unparalleled in the history of human thought. The Second Part of the Summa Theologica is a masterly exposition of the internal workings of the human mind: what motivates, what hinders, what develops, what colors, what enlightens, what darkens, and what determines human behavior—in all its phases, in all of its choices, in every human circumstance. And what strengthens, what assists, what directs, what supports and what saves human behavior from making dangerous and unhealthy choices.

Father Flanagan's training in psychology, in the deepest and most penetrating meaning of the word, was far superior to anything available in any university of the day, and the Treatise on Man in the First Part of the Summa Theologica and the Second Part on human behavior have never been surpassed by any other thinker, before or since. It is clinical in its examination of human behavior in the whole range of human choices, and demonstrates vividly the height of human excellence and the depths of human depravity open to human beings. It can truly be called, not only a Summa Theologica, but a Summa Psychologica as well, and is the first major study of what might be called "normative anthropology".

It is not a narrow study of the panorama of human emotions that influence and condition human behavior. It categorizes, codifies, analyzes and identifies the rich contribution of the emotions in the life of human beings, and how the scope and tenor of human emotions are a major factor in physical, mental and emotional health. So Edward Flanagan, like his patron, St. John Bosco, had not only a vast and unprecedented experiential knowledge of the adolescent boy from his experience on the streets and from his valuable research on the men of his Workingmen's Hotel, where he sheltered thousands of broken men whose boyhood had been shattered by homelessness and neglect. He had a well-pondered and intellectual understanding long before Freud, Jung and Adler came on the scene with their theories and insights. From the heart of his own work, he was equipped to critique them and draw from them whatever valid insights they could throw upon his own work.

Because, like St. Thomas, he was open to the valid and demonstrable conclusions of any genuine human science, he could learn from a wide variety of experts in any professional field and was not closed to correcting some of his own conclusions when there was ample scientific evidence. However, he had developed a highly critical mind and he knew how to separate the true from the false, the credible from the unproved.

He would certainly have applauded and followed St. Thomas's insight that "to inquire into the meaning of animal is one thing; to inquire into the meaning of the human animal is quite another". It was the human person, created in the image of God, with a dignity and individuality that was sacred to each one that guided him in his life's work, and he never lost respect and reverence for the uniqueness of every boy who came to him. Somehow that seemed to rub off on even the toughest lads who came through his door, as they tried to live up to the exalted image he gave them of themselves.

He got his first glimpses of social injustice and its consequences in the writings of Charles Dickens and he always looked upon Dickens as a master of his craft: the highlighting and ferreting out of social evils and pursuing them until they were exposed in all their ugliness.

He had grasped very early the real meaning of the priestly vocation and priestly holiness, and he pursued both with an energy and relentlessness that almost burned him out before his journey had scarcely begun. It was no conventional view and he did not get it from manuals of piety or ascetical treatises. He got it from a companionship with his Maker that was developed in the long hours tending his father's sheep, with a book in his hand and a Rosary in his pocket. He had acquired something in those long stretches of aloneness that no seminary could have taught him: that priestly holiness means living under the very gaze of God. His ancient forebears in Early Ireland called it "the hovering of God" and it fostered several generations of "saints and scholars" who transformed the world they lived in. Somehow a young boy with his books and beads on the peat bogs and flowering heather of Ireland, captured a like vision and left behind a legacy as notable as theirs.

The Last Time I Saw Him

In February of 1948, I was studying for the priesthood at the Trappist Monastery of New Melleray in Dubuque, Iowa and had been there for almost two years when Father Flanagan came to see me. He had had a speaking engagement in Clinton, Iowa, south of Dubuque, and the Prior of the monastery was going to pick him up. I was to serve his Mass in the morning and would talk over breakfast with him in the guesthouse, and afterwards have a long visit in the Bishop's room of the monastery. It was almost six years to the day since I had first met him.

He came into the church, tall and stately as I remembered him, but looking very tired. He was glad to see me and I could see that he was proud that one of his boys was a Trappist. I think he felt that I was a substitute for him, since he had tried several times to enter the Trappists in Gethsemani Abbey in Kentucky, but had been refused permission each time by his bishop. Now one of his Boys Town graduates would wear the white robe of the Trappist in his place. I knew that my being at New Melleray made him happy and that added to my happiness in being there.

He told me about his trip to Japan and Korea at the request of General Douglas MacArthur, and I learned later other details from the Report he had written for General MacArthur after his trip. It was a terrible, harrowing experience for him, as he saw boys and girls in Japan and Korea banded together like animals and victimized by profiteering adults who were paid handsomely by the government for setting up youth centers, but who spent only a fraction of what they received on the actual care of their charges. The trip had depressed and sickened him, and in his Report, he lashed out in anger at those who profited from the sufferings of innocent children.

He spoke movingly of Boys Town and how he would like to remain there and watch the building off the new Boys Town. A whole new Boys Town was underway and he wanted to be there. All the dreams he had shared with us at those 11 o'clock conferences were becoming a reality. The fields to the east where we used to play saw a new City of Little Men being built as streets were laid out and buildings starting to rise.

"I would like to stay at Boys Town," he said, "but the President and the State Department have asked me to go to Europe and do the same thing I did in the Far East. How can I refuse the President of the United States?"

He could not, of course. He had to go. It was not a youth in trouble in some juvenile court or some boy from a broken home asking to come to Boys Town. It was a whole generation of German and French and Italian youths who were in trouble, and very literally, he was the only one who could help them. This he knew very well, but he was not sure he would survive the trip.

Riding to the monastery from Clinton, he had said to Father Vincent, the prior. "I have one comfort in all this. There is a new Boys Town now with room for a thousand boys. I can go to my rest in peace."

"You're not thinking of leaving us, are you, Monsignor?" the prior asked, wondering exactly what he meant.

"Oh, I'm not kidding myself," Father Flanagan said. "I don't have much time left." We talked long into the morning. When the prior came to take him to the train for Omaha, he gave me his blessing, said he would see me again when he returned from Europe. I had asked him about a few of my classmates, and he promised to send me their addresses.

That was the last time I saw him.

As Eddie Dunn, the young mayor of Boys Town said Goodbye to him at the Omaha airport, he had never seen Father Flanagan so tired.

"Come back soon," he said. "Graduation this year will be in our new auditorium and you'll have to be there."

"I haven't missed a graduation yet," said Father Flanagan. "I'll see you in the spring."

At Vatican City, Father Flanagan had a long and earnest talk with Pope Pius XII, and managed a long visit with an old friend and classmate, Monsignor Enrico Dante, now the papal Prefect of Ceremonies. He also took time to see his old classroom in the Gregorian University where he had studied forty years before. Then he flew to Germany. As in Japan, there was a frenzied schedule of meetings with government officials and military authorities. And everywhere, there were boys.

As the picture of postwar Europe unfolded before him, the situation in Germany seemed critical. The young people of the whole nation had been deeply indoctrinated with Nazism and it would take many long years to erase the effects from their minds. On all sides, too, was the growing threat of Communism. The rebuilding of Europe threatened to be more difficult than the rebuilding of the Orient.

The weary priest saw the misery of the wartorn cities and the thousands of hungry and homeless children.

"There is so much to be done," he told his nephew, Pat Norton, who accompanied him, "and so little time. A hundred Boys Towns would not be enough to care for all these children. How I wish I were fifty years younger."

As his heart sank in Italy and broke in Germany, he did not know that another Irish priest, inspired by his example, was already building Boys Towns that would become famous in their own right. Monsignor John Carroll-Abbing would multiply his Boy Republics throughout Italy and would transplant the vision and principles of Father Flanagan to the soil of the Old World.

In Berlin, Father Flanagan's schedule called for a series of long conferences, in addition to his visit to a boys' home that was thought to be the beginning of a Boys Town in Germany. It was sponsored by the Air Force, and a former Boys Town citizen had a large hand in its creation.

With the meetings and conferences over, Father Flanagan went with a company of Air Force officers to the boy's home on the second floor of a large building in downtown Berlin. It was evident that he was worn out even before he started to climb a long flight of stairs. At the top step, he stopped, exhausted. He turned pale and was breathing heavily.

"What's the matter, Father?" one of the young officers asked him.

"I can scarcely move, he said. Then suddenly straightening up, he added: "But I have to look my best, the boys are waiting."

He spent the rest of the day in conversation with Cardinal Von Preysing of Berlin, who was an old classmate from Innsbruck University, where they both had studied, and they talked about the wrecked lives and wrecked cities around them. As student in the seminary, they had climbed Alpine peaks together, and they reminisced on those happy, quiet days when ordination to the priesthood was their dream and their goal.

Before going to bed, Father Flanagan looked at his next day's schedule: a meeting with General Lucius Clay, the American Commander, and then a meeting with German youth leaders, who were eager to hear his views on the youth problems of their country.

But the strain and labor had been too much. In the middle of the night, he was rushed to a Berlin Army Hospital. A few hours later, his great, wonderful heart gave out, and the friend and builder of boys was dead.

When the abbot of the monastery called me in and told me about Father Flanagan's death, I went out and walked under the trees and wondered what Boys Town would be like without him. A light had gone out of my sky. Father Flanagan was dead.

I sat down and wrote a poem in his memory, pouring into it all that I had felt for the man and all that I owed him as a priest, a father and a friend. I would never see him again and he would never see Boys Town again. At Boys Town, a newly-ordained priest, Father Jack Farrald, was waiting for him to come home to celebrate his first Mass. Instead, he would take part in his funeral.

He had asked to be buried on the green hill that slopes down from Boys Town to the great open meadow in front of the town, but room was made for him in a small crypt at the side of the chapel. Later, a great shrine was being built where he rests today.

In my poem, I tried to capture something of his vision and his spirit as I remembered and experienced it.

To Father Flanagan (May 15, 1948)

-I-

You saw the empty hulks pour through your doors.
You gave them food and tried to give them more.
They sat and stared at you, dead to their cores,
And went away as empty as before.

Misshapen ore that could not be re-formed,
These empty lives, they never could be filled.
For though the man was fed, the body warmed,
The heart and mind and soul of him were killed.

A street, a dirty face, an impish grin,
A ray of Godness shining through a lad;
You saw him and you took him, took him in,
And gave him all you were and all you had.

"'Give him a field to run in, God knows, he was made to run;
And give him the wind and the prairies and a spot beneath the sun.
Give him stuff for his hands to shape and things for his heart to love,
Then leave him alone to God alone and the dreams he is dreaming of."

-II-

You took this tired life, this light yet dim,
And poured on it the light and love of truth.
You planted, watered, weeded, prayed o'er him,
And shot a shot of glory through the youth.

This bent and clouded life reached out anew
To stars and roads and horizonic things;
He found new worlds to conquer and to hew,
And learnt in smithies how the anvil rings.

A thousand streets, a thousand streets and more,
A thousand alleyways and country lanes,
A thousand lads from Nome to Singapore
Haw learned to know your face and speak your name.

Somewhere in a German town the stars rolled back their doors,
And hands that molded seas and suns reached down and folded yours.
Deep in the wings of God you slept, tired and weary so.
You were one of earth's greatest and someday the world will know.

Printed in the United States
By Bookmasters